This book belongs to:

For Stew

First published 2023 by Walker Books Ltd
87 Vauxhall Walk, London SE11 5HJ

2 4 6 8 10 9 7 5 3 1

This book has been typeset in Avenir

Printed in China

British Library Cataloguing in Publication Data:
a catalogue record for this book is available from the British Library

ISBN 978-1-5295-0910-6

www.walker.co.uk

Yippee! Rabbit

Jo Ham

WALKER BOOKS
AND SUBSIDIARIES
LONDON • BOSTON • SYDNEY • AUCKLAND

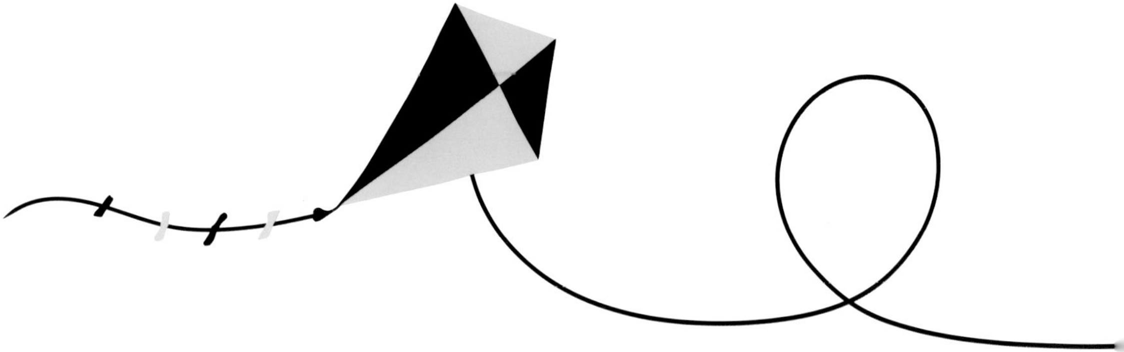

Rabbit go

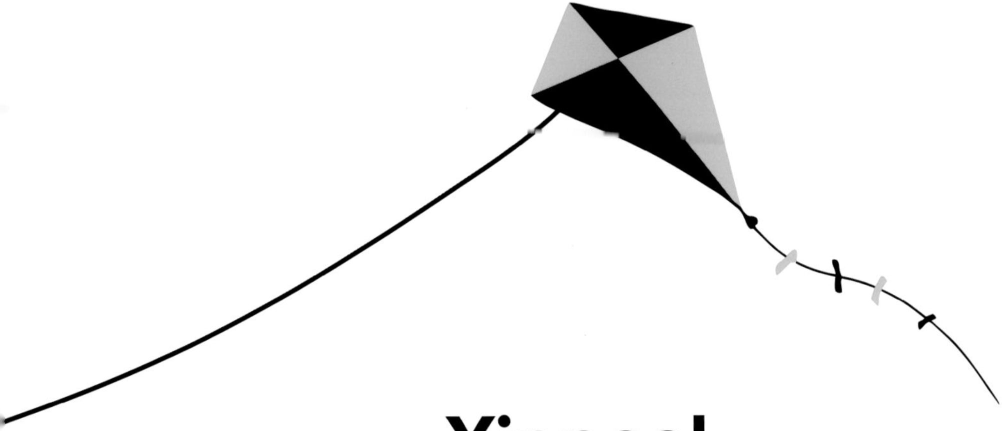

Yippee!

Rabbit stop

Rabbit go

Yippee!

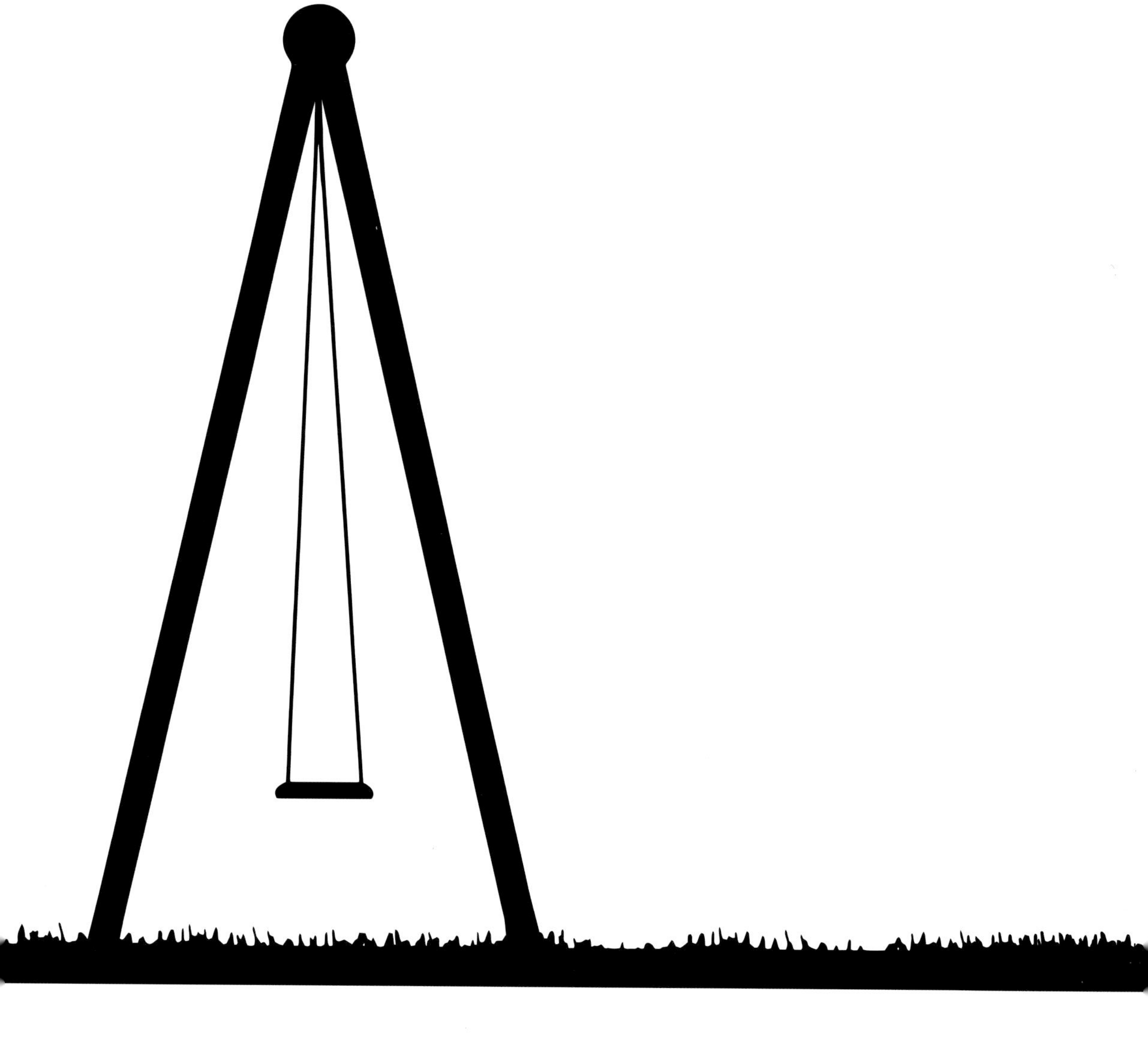

Rabbit stop

Rabbit go

Yippee!

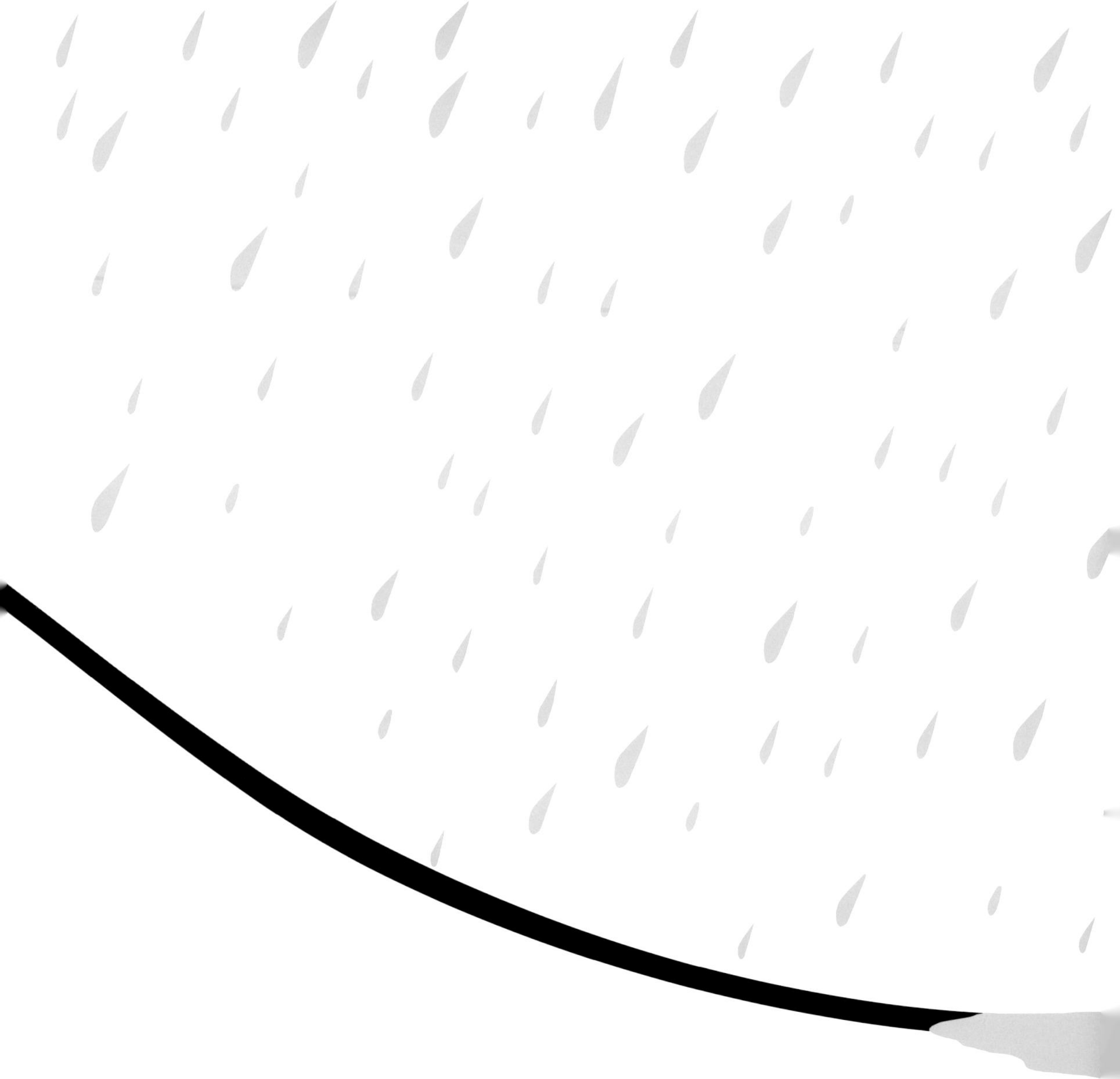

Rabbit stop

Rabbit go

Yippee!

Rabbit GO!